Arthur Loveless

Celebrating a Seattle Architectural Legacy

Susan Shorett
Christine Tyler
Photography by Eric Dennon

Copyright 2024 Susan Shorett, Christine Tyler, and Eric Dennon

Photography © Eric Dennon

All rights reserved. No part of this book may be reproduced or transmitted in any form or by any means, electronic or mechanical, including photocopying, recording, or by any information storage and retrieval system, without written permission from the authors, except for the inclusion of brief quotations in a review.

Published by Susan Shorett and Christine Tyler
Arthur Loveless: Celebrating a Seattle Architectural Legacy

ISBN 979-8-218-24690-7

Cover design by Phil Kovacevich
Additional Design and Editing, Proofreading by Shauna Naf

Printed in USA

For permission requests, contact the publisher at: shorettgroup@gmail.com

The events and in this book have been recorded based on the information and research available via recollections and stories of others, historical documentation, and public records. The authors would be pleased to make good any omissions or rectify any mistakes brought to their attention at the earliest opportunity.

Visit www.ArthurLoveless.com for more information about the authors, upcoming events and releases.

We would like to thank 4Culture for the grant that was awarded to our Loveless book project. 4Culture is cultural funding agency for King County who works to make our region vibrant in public art, preservation, art and heritage to support the intersecting and evolving disciplines, forms, and places where culture is expressed and experienced. Historic Preservation is supporting the preservation of the historic places that give King County its character.

Thanks also to our granting partner, the Southwest Seattle Historical Society.

Table of Contents

9   Introduction:
       Arthur Loveless Biography

16   Arthur Loveless Projects Map

Public Works

20   Loveless Studio Building

30   University of Washington Greek Row

36   Washington Park Arboretum Gate

38   W.T. Campbell Building

40   Colman Pool

42   Brighton Presbyterian Church

Residential Designs

WEST SEATTLE/MAGNOLIA/QUEEN ANNE

46   Colman Residence

52   John B. Shorett Residence

56   Clayton Wilson Residence

60   Fauntleroy Classic Brick Tudor

66   Florence Rice Residence

70   Dana & Jeannette Brown Residence

74   King/Wells Residence

78   Magnolia Bungalow

82   Sparkman Residence

BROADMOOR/CAPITOL HILL

90   Anderson Residence

96   Bloch Residence

WASHINGTON PARK/SEWARD PARK/
MT. BAKER

- 104 Corbet Residence
- 110 Eckstrom/Canning Residence
- 114 Brady Residence
- 118 Yates Hickey Residence
- 122 Palmer Residence
- 128 Pope Residence
- 134 Arthur Loveless Residence
- 140 John A. Porter Residence
- 144 Kinzer Residence
- 148 Bowles Residence
- 152 Loveless Gould Remodel

WINDERMERE/ LAURELHURST

- 158 Field Residence
- 164 Roebke Residence
- 170 Scripps Residence
- 174 Pierce Residence
- 178 Windermere Tudor Revival
- 184 Franklin Residence

VIEW RIDGE/SHERIDAN HEIGHTS

- 190 Shelton Residence
- 194 Street of Dreams

EDMONDS/BAINBRIDGE ISLAND

- 200 Bloxon Residence
- 206 Frederick and Lucille Fischer Residence

- 212 About the Authors and Contributors

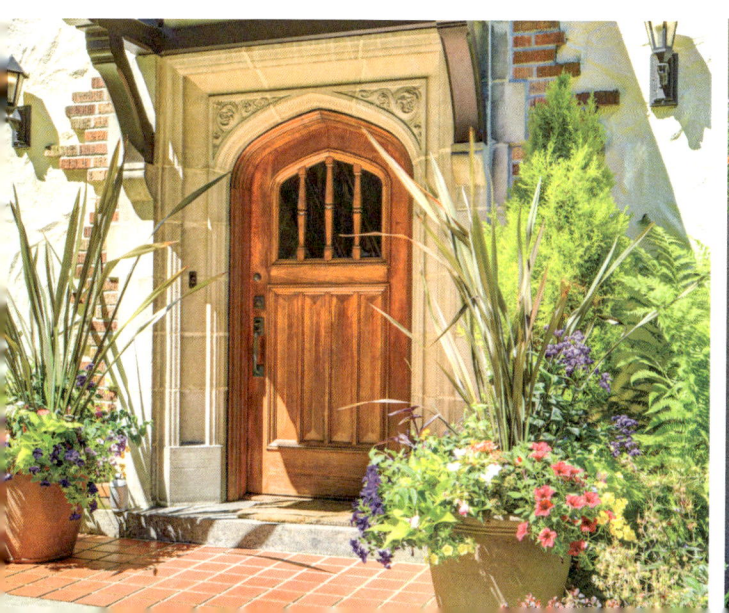

About this book

This book is a family affair.

Tina Tyler is the great-niece of Arthur Loveless and Susan Shorett is the great-great-niece of Arthur Loveless.

This collection of Arthur Loveless homes started out as family genealogy research endeavor. Both Susan and Tina have a love of history and passion for ancestry. The Loveless Building had been in their family until the late 1970's which was the starting point of their research. Their project began to change as they realized the full extent of the body of work produced by Loveless, and that there was no known comprehensive catalog of his work. Starting with Loveless design materials on file at the University of Washington's Special Collections and the UW Architectural Department Library, they spent additional, extensive time combing through the King Country Regional Archives, Washington State Archives, and Seattle Times Archives dating back from 1908 through 1970 to verify and curate a list of homes and commercial buildings designed by Loveless or in conjunction with a partner. To date, this is the most comprehensive list of Loveless designs. Older family members and family records also added to the research.

Once they had compiled a comprehensive list of Loveless designs, they reached out to current homeowners with the idea of photographing and documenting the long lasting and ongoing influence of Arthur Loveless. Homeowner cooperation and support has made this book possible. There is also a sense of preservation urgency. Since 2017, five Loveless homes have been demolished, and others are at risk due to the growth of the area and the scenic location of many of the homes. Tina and Susan decided to document and honor the legacy of their relative in the form of this color paged book and partner with the Southwest Seattle Historical Society to further their project.

Eric Dennon is a real estate photographer with experience in editorial HD photography, aerial drone photography and videography. He has shot thousands of homes in the Pacific Northwest and focused on many of the quality materials and design details that Loveless was known for and to showcase the design influence that Loveless contributed to every established neighborhood in the Seattle area including the Arboretum, University of Washington and more.

Introduction

Arthur Loveless was a prolific, award-winning architect who made a significant architectural impact on every major Seattle neighborhood from 1907 to 1940. Over a near 40-year career span, Loveless developed a diverse and extensive body of work featuring over 100 properties. His residential work helped create the character of many Seattle neighborhoods, including West Seattle, Magnolia, Capitol Hill, Queen Anne, Washington Park, Madison Park, Seward Park, Broadmoor, Leschi, Madrona, Mount Baker, Laurelhurst, and Windermere. He designed both commercial community settings and private resident homes including seven University of Washington Greek Row sororities and fraternities – more than any other architect to date. He designed the gatehouse at the Washington Park Arboretum and the original Seattle Repertory Playhouse. The most distinctive and well-known of his structures is the Loveless Building located at the north end of Capitol Hill that continues to serve the local community today with retail, restaurants, and apartments.

As his reputation grew, Loveless was hired by many prominent residents of the city to design their personal residences including the Dexter Horton mansion, the Colman mansion, the Pantages mansion, the John Porter residence, the Darrah Corbet residence, and nearly sixty additional homes in Seattle neighborhoods.

In addition to his architectural accomplishments, Loveless was a prominent patron of the arts in Seattle and a sponsor/supporter of artists locally and internationally. He was a world traveler, collector, gardener, photographer and philanthropist.

Arthur Loveless was born on September 22, 1873, in Big Rapids, Michigan. His parents, Loren and Caroline Loveless, had two children, Arthur and Georgia. Even as a youth, Arthur showed an interest in photography and drama. After high school he worked at a bank until an architectural lecture series created as a correspondence course by the University of Chicago caught his eye. The course nurtured his interest in the field and in 1902, he enrolled in the architectural department at Columbia University in New York City. Although he is often shown as having graduated in the Class of 1905, he ran out of funds before graduating. He took an apprenticeship position with one of his teachers, William Adams Delano of Delano & Aldrich, a firm that became well known throughout the country for the design of stately eclectic homes from which Loveless could add to his resume.

In 1907, Arthur came to Seattle at the encouragement of his sister, Georgia, and her husband, John B. Shorett, a prominent Seattle attorney. Loveless joined up with Clayton D. Wilson as the chief draftsman in the partnership of Wilson & Loveless. In addition to designing Wilson's own home, the firm designed homes for Arthur's sister Georgia, William Bloch in 1908 and J. K. Sparkman and H.R. Kennedy in 1909. The firm is best known for designing in 1909 the personal home of Alexander Pantages, who owned a string of theaters on the West Coast. All these homes were designed with neoclassical elements and still exist today.

In 1912, Loveless opened his own firm with an office at the Colman Building in downtown Seattle. It was there he became acquainted with prominent philanthropist Lawrence Colman. There began a longtime collaboration, starting with a lobby remodel of the Colman Building. This continued with a private residence for Colman, the Colman Pool, and the first eight lots in the new development of Windermere. He also designed several homes in the Colman-Denny tract known as Laurelhurst. In 1923, he joined four other investors to buy and develop a ten-acre parcel for five homes on Lake Washington in Seward Park known as the Carraher Tract. Plans included Loveless's personal residence, named 'Hollyhock House.'

Lester Fey joined Loveless as an associate in the late early 1930s. Fey worked himself up from the position of chief draftsman to become a full partner in the firm of Loveless and Fey. They worked together until Loveless's retirement in 1940.

In the late 1930's he joined with several other prominent architects including Edwin Ivey, William Bain, George W. Stoddard and J. Lister Holmes to design homes for a "Street of Dreams" project in Sheridan Heights. Sponsored by the Bon Marche Department Store, Puget Mill Company and Seattle Trust and Savings Bank, the homes were designed to showcase new building techniques and materials in homebuilding (including "crack-less" walls), to reflect the unique and new Pacific Northwest culture and promote development of the Sheridan Beach area.

As he neared retirement from his architectural practice, he sold his beloved "Hollyhock House" in Seward Park and moved to a two-story unit in his Loveless Building in 1938. Following retirement in 1940, he lived there as

Zeta Psi fraternity, University of Washington, Seattle, University of Washington Libraries, Special Collections, UW 19589

The Colman Building

Loveless residence, University of Washington Libraries, Special Collections, UW 41365

University of Washington Repertory Theater

Loveless Studio Building, University of Washington Libraries, Special Collections, UW 41363

he traveled and participated in local events until his death in 1971. He was ninety-seven years old. He never married or had any children. He left his estate to his sister Georgia's children—four nephews and nieces. One nephew, La Monte Shorett, followed his uncle into the architectural field.

Throughout his career, Arthur Loveless was very active in the American Institutes of Architects. In 1913 he was admitted to the Washington State Chapter of the American Institute of Architects. In 1914 he was elected secretary and less than two years later he became president of the chapter. Active in the leadership, he was reelected several times as president but relinquished his position as he neared retirement and the onset of WWII. Loveless was made a Fellow in 1941. The citation read "for his contribution to the profession in the field of domestic architecture and for the uniform excellence of his design and executed work." He received a variety of recognitions and architectural awards including awards for the designs for the Darrah Corbet house, Zeta Psi Fraternity, and the Loveless Building.

Loveless's distinctive style and quality craftsmanship influenced other builders and architects of his era. His most influential style was Tudor Revival, although he also designed in other styles, such as neoclassical,

Spanish colonial, French Norman revival, and, in later years, American colonial. Frederick Anhalt was influenced by Loveless as he started out as a draftsman for Loveless and subsequently became an independent builder of apartments with very similar details to those Loveless incorporated into his designs. Many architects today consider Loveless one of the most influential architects of

John Porter Residence, University of Washington Libraries, Special Collections, UW 13396

his time in Seattle. The impact of his distinctive style, elements of his usage of space, and the volume of work created a lasting imprint on the neighborhoods where his creations are located. Loveless paid particular attention to the site position of each home, the juxtaposition of the views, and the quality of materials and craftsmanship. He was mindful of the placement of rooms to consider the views. Some of his residential designs are positioned "backwards" in layout, with formal living and dining rooms at the back of the home to take in the views while the street-side entrances are the least grand. Many of the front-door entrances of some of the largest homes were of modest English Cottage scale, yet with quality materials and highly detailed. He designed many large estate properties with intricate details and features such as hand-carved motif handrails, quarter-sawn oak, detailed tile motifs, built-in shelving, hidden rooms, and elaborate stained-glass windows. He considered the user's whole experience and featured high-quality materials that he often hand selected.

As Loveless's architecture practice and recognition grew, his projects were often announced in the Seattle Times' society pages, as was his participation in travel and arts events. Upon his arrival in Seattle, he joined the Mountaineers and become a patron of the fine arts.

His first mention in the Times was in 1908, when he entered an architectural contest for the local AIA. Upon return from his world travels, he would be a frequent presenter at the University Women's Club. In May 1913, the paper reported that he was a guest at a gala thrown by the Seattle Arts Association, and the next month he served on a committee hosting a flower show in West Seattle. Loveless's activities on the local cultural scene included reviewing garden books for the local Cultural Society, judge for a local architectural design contest, and attending fundraisers for the Seattle Symphony, the Moore Theatre and premiers of plays at the Seattle Repertory Theatre. He was elected to the board of directors for the Pacific Northwest Academy of Arts. He was a founding member of Pro Musica as well as the Capitol Commerce Club. 'Hollyhock House,' his personal Lake Washington waterfront residence in Seward Park, was a stop on the Junior League Garden tour in 1925. The gardens were designed by the Olmsted brothers, whose family had designed New York's Central Park. The brothers were friends with Loveless and had collaborated on gardens for several of his commissioned designs. Loveless was also acquainted with, and an active supporter of Nellie Cornish, of the Cornish School of Dance. He designed the residence of Mary Ann Wells, a dance instructor at the school.

Loveless had an avid interest in supporting artists in many fields. He designed the Studio Building, later renamed the Loveless Building, to support local artists by providing street level studios with 10 apartments accessed through an inner courtyard where the artists could live. He sponsored and supported artists both local and international. Among the latter was Mohamed Drisi, whom Loveless discovered while traveling in Morocco. His support sent the Téruan-born Drisi to the Julio Briedo Art School in Spain. Drisi's painting career included a commission to paint a portrait of Princess Grace of Monaco, which was used on an official national stamp, and he eventually opened his well-known gallery in Chicago that is still open today.

In addition to supporting the arts, Loveless had a keen interest in international travel starting in the mid-1930s. His trips grew more frequent after he retired around 1940 and continued into the 1960s. Most international travel during that period included long ship passages and shorter plane trips. Loveless's major trips lasted anywhere from six to twelve months and got longer after he retired.

He ventured to Mexico to study the country's art and architecture in 1937. In 1938, he journeyed to Hawaii aboard the SS Empress of Japan, then ventured to Malaya, Bora-Bora, Samoa, and eventually Borneo. This was just prior to the Japanese invasion of the Pacific during World War II, and Loveless took films of his journeys that he presented at local society lectures. Loveless was a favorite speaker at the University Women's Club, the College Club and other groups as he shared his films and pictures of his travels: 1938 College Club on color films of Mexican art and architecture; 1941 lecture on Bali and Java to the Washington State Music Teachers Association; a fundraiser for British American War Relief, Madrona Chapter, sponsored by the Seattle Art Museum and UW Anthropology Department; and a 1941 travelogue to the science and travel classes of University Women's Club on Burma and Peking. In 1946 he bought a house in Morelia, Mexico, to share with family members. He also

Arthur Loveless in Madrid with Juan Prieto, an artist from Spain. Loveless sponsored the artist, Mohamed Drisi, allowing him to attend Prieto's school and later sponsored him for admittance to the U.S.

traveled to Central and South America, including Ecuador and Nicaragua, and Guatemala. In 1949 Loveless traveled first-class from New York City to Barcelona, Spain, aboard the SS Atlantic. In subsequent years he toured most of Europe as well as Malta, Morocco, and Tangiers. In January 1963, the Seattle Times noted that Loveless had returned to Seattle from his fifth trip to China. He made six trips there altogether before China was closed to Westerners in the late 1960s. Many of his home movies and photos of his travels were donated to the University of Washington library. He was an award-winning amateur photographer taking 2nd place in a Saturday Review contest for his photo "Ballet" taken of Penang, Malaysian fishermen pulling in their nets.

Through his travels, he amassed a significant collection of antiquities, including many from China: snuff bottles, porcelain vases, rosewood furniture, porcelain screens, jade bowls and figurines, ivory statues, wood carvings, a belt buckle collection, and silk fabrics. He donated a significant Chinese snuff bottle collection to the Seattle Art Museum in the 1960s. In 1963 he donated over 90 pieces of historic textiles and ceremonial fabrics from Guatemala to the newly created Fine Textile Museum at the University of Washington (later MOHAI). He first photographed them on local residents, then curated them in an attempt to preserve the anthropological value of vanishing custom textiles. The photographs were donated as well.

From architect to world traveler and collector, Arthur Loveless's civic engagement had impact on Seattle through his architectural achievements, arts and cultural participation, and his philanthropic donations that added to the early development of Seattle. Many public buildings continue to be in use, and many of his homes are still identified by the names of their original owners with their current owners often striving to preserve the hallmark elements of a Loveless-design structure. With the immense pressure on land re-development in Seattle, preservation of his architectural contributions continue to be at risk. Since 2017, five of his designed structures have been demolished, with many more before that. With a documented body of work of over 120 structures, his work deserves to be recognized and preserved. This book is dedicated to his work and the search continues for documentation of additional Loveless designed homes and cultural contributions.

Arthur Loveless Projects

● Indicates buildings featured in this book
● Indicates known Loveless home
● Indicates demolished Loveless home

Public Works

Loveless Studio Building

1924-1930

CAPITOL HILL NEIGHBORHOOD

This historic building was first known as the Studio Building. It was one of the first of its kind for the intended use in Seattle. Loveless designed the building as a work/live shared space for artists, a concept found more common in Europe, and one he wanted to promote as he was a supporter of local arts and artists. The artists could work in the street-front "studios" and live in the ten apartments located upstairs by entering through an interior courtyard. Loveless purchased the land in 1924 which is located at the corner of Roy and Broadway and completed the building in 1930. From the street side retail section, arched windows with stone and wood detailing are most identifiable. From the interior courtyard, a fountain is the centerpiece surrounded by mature landscaping. Each apartment is different in layout and entrance. A turreted entrance, dormer windows, stained glass windows and efficient kitchens vary from unit to unit, and all face the courtyard. Loveless designed a corner unit for himself, first as his office and then later after he retired and sold his home, he lived there and kept many of his antiquity collections in his office.

Today, the building remains a vibrant destination for community experiences of both retail shopping and dining on the street side, plus rental housing in the ten apartments accessed through the courtyard. The charming details of the English style stone building continue to define the character of the north end of Capitol Hill on Broadway. Because of the Depression, some of the building materials were altered – for instance, some of the intended stone was replace by concrete poured to look like stone. The structure was cited in 1961 by the Seattle Chapter, American Institute of Architecture, as an older building of enduring quality.

The Loveless building is the distinctive anchor at the heart of the north end of Capitol Hill. With retail, restaurant and residential living, it continues to be a thriving asset to the neighborhood and community.

The interior courtyard of the Loveless Building provides access to the apartments.

Above: Interior staircase to the upstairs "studio" apartments.

Right: Entrance to corner unit that Loveless used as his architectural office and later his personal residence.

Left: Stained glass insert highlights a contractor working with a trowel for lath and plaster application.

Bottom Left: The stained glass insert inside the leaded glass window highlights a construction man working with a saw.

Bottom Right: From an interior position inside one of the Loveless apartments looking out towards the courtyard.

The Russian Samovar Tea Room: At the Loveless Building

The restaurant space in the Loveless Building originally housed a tea room. Called the 'Russian Samovar' it opened in 1931, featuring hand-painted wood wall murals by Vladimir Shkurkin. The murals depicted Russian fairy tales from the poem, "Tale of Czar Salton" written by A.S. Pushkin. Over the years, the original murals became sun faded and eventually a restaurateur covered them over in a later remodel. Those murals have recently been discovered intact under additional wall coverings and have been restored for the public to enjoy.

Subsequent restaurants, booksellers, coffee and retail shops continue to be anchors that draw the attention of the community.

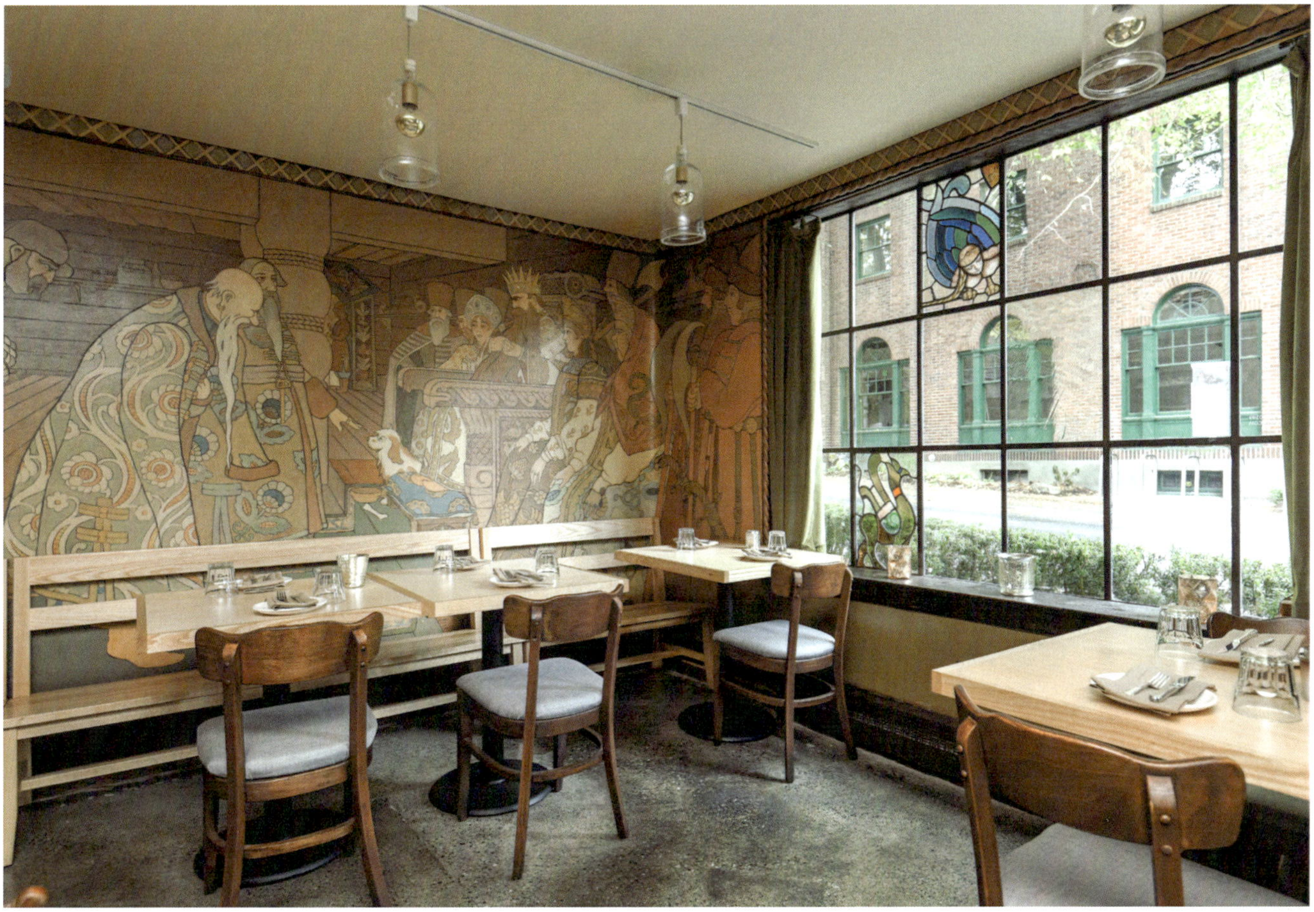

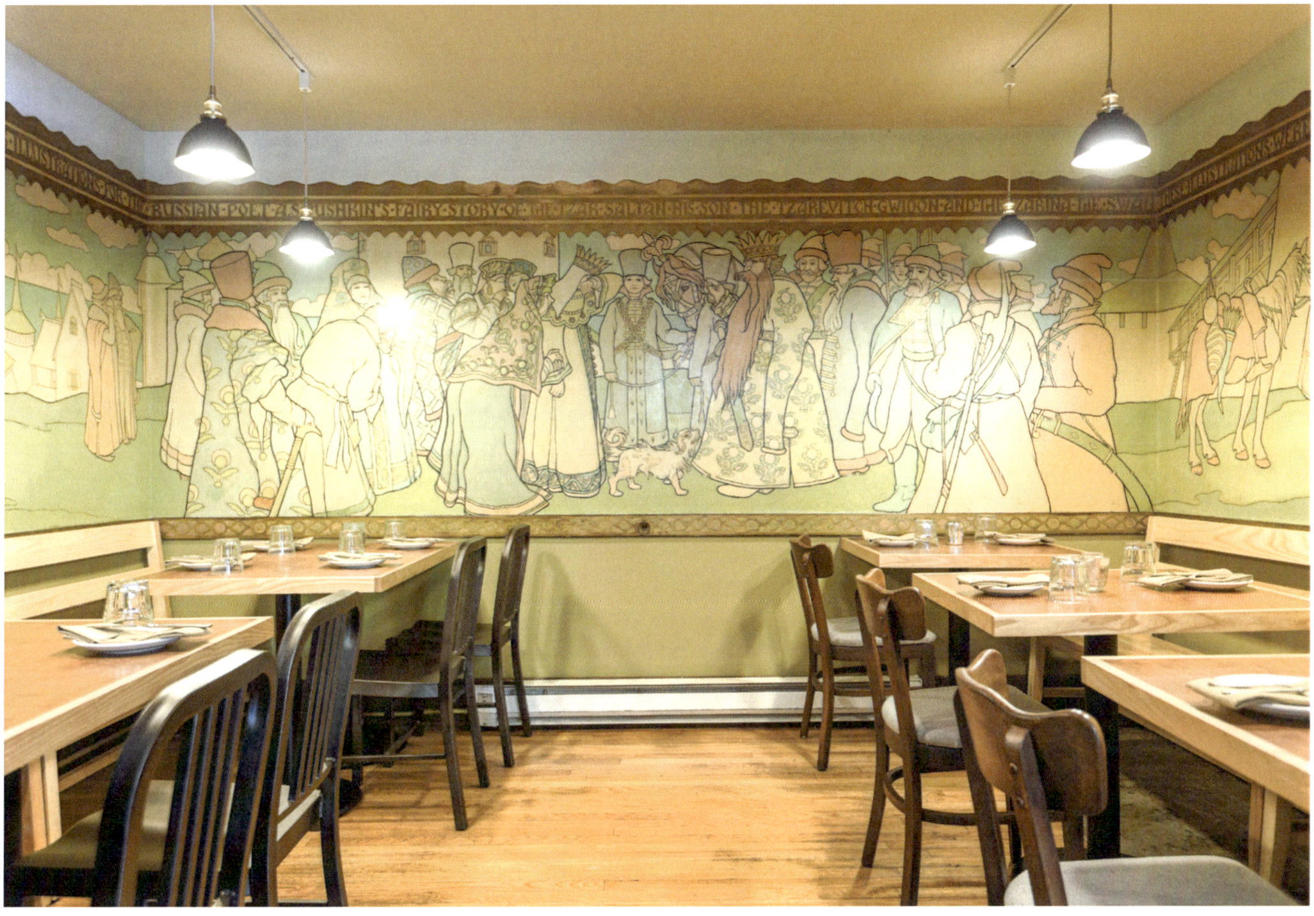
ILLUSTRATIONS FOR
RUSSIAN POET
FAIRY STORY OF
SON THE TZAREVITCH GWIDON AND

University of Washington Greek Row

UNIVERSITY DISTRICT NEIGHBORHOOD

Arthur Loveless designed more University of Washington Greek Row homes than any other architecture firm. While some have been extensively remodeled over the years, the influence of his designs helped shape the style and overall image of UW's Greek Row which is still vibrant and active today. Many of the buildings have undergone frequent remodels to modernize and adapt to the needs of the students yet some of the original architectural details are still in evidence. Several have changed chapter affiliations over time.

Alpha Gamma Delta: Designed in 1923 this sorority was on 4515 21st and estimated to cost $30,000 to build. In 1936, the house was put on rollers and taken across the street to become the Phi Sigma Kappa house at 2104 NE 45th. It is now the home of Evans Scholars of Washington. (Alpha Gamma Delta now is in a modern building next door.)

Alpha Xi Delta: Designed in 1923, this sorority is on 4522 18th Ave NE and estimated to cost $25,000 to build. It is now Theta Xi fraternity. It was identified through drawings in the Arthur Loveless Special Collections at the UW Library as the exterior has retained the original style.

Alpha Theta Delta: Designed in 1924, this is now Alpha Epsilon Pi at 4541 19th Ave NE. The roof line and upper gabled windows retain some of the original design elements, but the entry has been heavily remodeled. Originally it would have been similar to Alpha Xi Delta.

Beta Theta Pi: Originally constructed in 1922 in a traditional Norman style with a gabled roof, it was remodeled in 1956, removing the gabled roof and the Norman elements to the point that the original Loveless style no longer exists.

Zeta Tau Alpha Sorority

Designed in 1929, the wrought iron balconies with French doors and brick and stone exterior with detailed trim are distinctly French Provincial.

Delta Gamma Sorority

This was the last of Greek Row homes designed by Loveless in 1936 in a traditional colonial style. Located at the corner of 21st and 45th with the entrance on 2012 NE 45th. The exterior remains remarkably close to the original design painted white with black trim, the house features a formal front entry and a courtyard on the side of the home.

Zeta Psi Fraternity

Designed in 1927, this building is in the English Tudor Gothic country style to resemble a hunting lodge and Loveless was awarded an AIA architecture award for the design of this fraternity. The brick façade with half-timber details are strong features of this building. Tudor stacked chimneys are also prominent details and a large wood front door. The large living room features high gabled ceilings. It is located on East 47th and 21st Ave NE. The building has retained many of the original features on the exterior of the building while there have been additions to the rear of the building.

Washington Park Arboretum Gate

1937

WASHINGTON PARK
NEIGHBORHOOD

The University of Washington hired Loveless and Fey to collaborate to design the Gatehouse entrance to the new Arboretum Park managed by the University of Washington. Originally built as part of an Entrance Lodge, everyone today who enters or exits the south entrance to Washington Park Arboretum passes through the entrance gate that Loveless designed in 1937. The entry sets the tone of the entire arboretum as a distinct and much-loved local public park. The original gatehouse was done in an English cottage style built of basaltic stone covered with moss to give the gates and building the appearance of age. It was built to balance the rock gardens where stones were set to look as if they occurred there naturally.

W.T. Campbell Building

1911

WEST SEATTLE NEIGHBORHOOD

W.T. Campbell was a teacher-turned real estate businessperson. He taught at the West Seattle Central and Brick Schools.

He made the strategic purchase of two lots on the corner of California Avenue and Ninth Street (now Alaska Street) in anticipation of the coming rail line and annexation and commissioned Wilson & Loveless to design the building. Campbell, himself, served as the builder.

Considered the most significant and recognizable "anchor" building and the heart of the West Seattle Alaska Junction district, the Campbell Building sets the tone of the character of this neighborhood. The West Seattle Historical Survey group has determined that the building is significant enough to be considered a grade A candidate for landmark preservation status. It continues to house both retail and business office space and has always been a commercial retail and office building throughout the decades.

Pictured right is the Campbell Building in its first decade or thereabouts.

In 2017, the Campbell Building received a Landmark designation. It was cited as "arguably West Seattle's most significant building as a deeply symbolic anchor at the center of The Junction, West Seattle's most prosperous commercial district."

MOHAI, PEMCO Webster & Stevens Collection, 1983.10.12198.1

Colman Pool
1941

WEST SEATTLE
NEIGHBORHOOD

Kenneth Colman engaged Loveless to design the Colman Pool in Lincoln Park as a memorial to his father Lawrence Colman. It was donated as a gift to the City of Seattle. Located on the idyllic beachfront in Lincoln Park, the saltwater swimming pool cost $100,000 to build. The pool design included a two diving boards, a clubhouse and locker rooms. Thousands of kids since the 1940s have spent hours at this pool and it continues to be an immensely popular community destination every summer.

Brighton Presbyterian Church

1927

SEWARD PARK
NEIGHBORHOOD

The 48,033 square foot, rectangular lot for this church is located between South Holly and South Willow Streets. This Tudor-styled church was first constructed in 1927 and faces eastwards onto 51st Avenue South. The north and side wings are the oldest parts of the church while the south wing is an addition. The church has mottled brick cladding with wood board siding in the gable end of the south wing. While fenestration varies, the north and side wings are characterized by rectangular lattice windows with a round window in the north gable end. The south wing primarily has casement windows. This church is an excellent example of how the Tudor architectural style was used during the early development of Seward Park. It retains many of its original features, including entryways, roofline, half-timbering, one-and-a-half story massing, and lattice windows. Therefore, it remains integral to the residential character of the Seward Park neighborhood.

Brighton Church has changed hands and religious faiths. Now a Synagogue, the original truss beams and stained glass windows remain.

The original altar was centered under a wooden arch that has been painted over. In the original section of the church, a door was removed yet original stained glass rosette window remains.

Residential Designs

West Seattle

Magnolia

Queen Anne

Colman Residence
1924

WEST SEATTLE NEIGHBORHOOD

Lawrence Colman was a wealthy Seattle businessman, financier, and philanthropist. The Colman Building, Colman pool, Colman docks are named after his family. Colman purchased 17 acres near the Fauntleroy Ferry dock which eventually became the Colman-Pierce property. Lawrence commissioned Loveless to build a grand 8100 square foot home on the property which he named "Laurentide." The property had extensive views of Lincoln Park and Vashon Island although the surrounding trees have partially impaired the view over the years. Loveless designed the home as an English Tudor style with textured stucco exterior, a heavy oak front door, sweeping pitched rooflines, and a shake roof. The home includes 8 bedrooms, 5 fireplaces throughout the house, 2 primary bedroom suites, upper-level servant staff quarters and an interior elevator. Building materials include white oak paneling, beamed ceilings, a carved grape leaf motif newel post staircase, Batchelder fireplace tiles and built-in bookcases. Lawrence Pierce, a subsequent heir of the home, developed a large rhododendron garden and installed greenhouses to the property that remain intact today.

The house remained in the Colman family until 2009 when the current owners purchased it and began updating the original systems; remodeling the kitchen and other rooms to restore the original grandeur of the home and restoring the garden and grounds.

Signature Loveless detailing at the Colman Mansion. Stucco and brick exterior with multiple tudor chimney stacks and a shake roof.

The home sits on 2.5 acres with award winning gardens.

Opposite: A signature Loveless entry door: Ornate carved wood and concrete tile design yet smaller in scale than some of his architectural contemporaries.

The detailed carved wood and tile fireplace in the living room is one of five fireplaces in the home.

Built-in glass bookcase, quarter sawn-oak paneling and a tile fireplace in grape leaf motif are features in the main study.

Opposite and Above: An ornate hand-carved oak staircase newel with a grape motif was hand selected by Loveless and serves as a focal point for the entry.

John B. Shorett Residence
1908

WEST SEATTLE NEIGHBORHOOD

Georgia Shorett was the younger sister of Arthur Loveless. She and her husband, John B. Shorett, moved to Seattle from Iowa around 1900. John Shorett was in the very first graduating law school class at the University of Washington in 1902. He practiced law as well as serving on several city departments including Parks and Recreation. Called 'the Father of the Duwamish,' he was the attorney for a group of businessmen, including William Boeing, who were interested in the development of the of the Duwamish River Valley as a viable industrial area. He became the President of the Seattle School Board until 1945. John and Georgia's four children inherited the estate of Arthur Loveless.

The house sits on a double lot designed for Georgia's extensive gardens and John's Iowa-style corn patch. The exterior is cedar siding. Today, other than a kitchen update, the house remains in near original condition. The interiors share similarity with other Loveless designs such as Clayton Wilson's home with the beamed ceiling, curved arched window casements and balustrades. The original butler's pantry is in between the kitchen and dining room.

Built in 1908 for his sister, Georgia Loveless Shorett, this is one of Loveless's first designs. The patterned cedar siding is original.

The double lot was designed for master gardening and has been lovingly maintained.

Opposite: Craftsman woodwork on staircase, French doors, built-in bench and box beams.

Classic details include beamed ceilings and arched window frames.

Clayton Wilson Residence
1908

WEST SEATTLE
NEIGHBORHOOD

Clayton Wilson was the first partner Loveless collaborated with after arriving in Seattle in 1907. Wilson and Loveless collaborated from 1908-1911 and designed the following buildings together:

- Campbell Building in 1911
- Public Safety Building for the City of Seattle in 1908
- Kennedy House in 1909
- Pantanges House in 1910
- Bloch House in 1908
- Rice House in 1910
- Shorett House 1908
- Wilson House in 1908
- And the Sparkman Residence in 1909

Designed for his partner Wilson, this West Seattle home has classic Craftsman details. Note the arched windows, wood balcony railings and pitched dormer roofline along with pocket doors with arched door frames, beamed ceilings and patterned hardwood floors

The triple wide front window is arched with three sets of casement windows and upper mullioned windows.

Rear exterior with stucco and half-timber detailing.

The wood throughout provides a feeling of warmth and cozy spaces.

Fauntleroy Classic Brick Tudor

1923

WEST SEATTLE NEIGHBORHOOD

Loveless designed many homes in the classic Tudor style. This home was designed in 1923 with a brick exterior, shake roof, pitched rooflines, and dormer windows. The property is located on a dead end street, bluff side, overlooking Fauntleroy Cove. The 3560 square foot home has a typical understated entry with 6 bedrooms and 3 bathrooms. The large-proportioned living room and dining room are positioned to take in the view of Puget Sound. Built-in bench seating in the living room offers wood detailing with equal focus on the stucco and tile fireplace. Built-ins also include bookshelves in the living room and dining cabinet in the dining room. The wrought-iron chandelier is original. A study next to the living room opens to a back deck that overlooks the backyard and pool. The kitchen has been updated into a modernized farmhouse kitchen. Upstairs rooms provide sweeping views overlooking Vashon Island.

This home in Fauntleroy sports both the original bannister as well as the curved front door. Also notice the original light sconce. This is a great example of an understated front door that Loveless was known for - an unassuming entrance leads the way to the understated elegance waiting within.

The living room features built-in book case, French doors, leaded paned windows and a built-in bench seat.

Built-in china hutch and original chandelier are features of the dining room.

Florence Rice Residence
1910

WEST SEATTLE
NEIGHBORHOOD

The original owner was William Rice. Rice was born in New York in 1844. He moved to Lewiston, Idaho, with wife Sarah around 1880, and was in farming. He at one time was the most prominent resident of northern Idaho. He was later engaged in the merchandising business and held a position of trust with John P. Vollmer and the Grostein & Binnard firm. Still later he served Nez Perce County two terms as probate judge, and at the expiration of his second term he and his family removed to where the town of Westlake now stands. Westlake was founded by Judge Rice, being named in honor of his wife, her maiden name being Westlake. After several years' residence there, Rice went to Seattle where he engaged in the grain business, which he conducted until his death. He left this home to his daughter Florence Rice, who never married and remained here until her death.

The house sits on a prominent street bluff-side with city views of the Seattle skyline. Originally, the house had wood cladding tall, mullioned windows, a clinker brick fireplace and built-in book cases. The house was heavily remodeled and the exterior covered in a "pebble-dash" treatment with aluminum windows. The original detailing removed except the oak quarter-sawn oak stair banisters which have carved panels.

Above: The Seattle skyline is a big feature of this bluff property.

The modest entry to this house has been altered significantly in its 100+ year history

Views of the Seattle skyline feature prominently throughout the house

Opposite: Original staircase and handrail designed by Wilson and Loveless.

Dana and Jeannette Brown Residence

1917

WEST SEATTLE NEIGHBORHOOD

Dana and Jeannette Brown moved to Seattle from Carson City NV in 1893. Dana was with the West Seattle Land & Improvement company and Jeannette was involved in several charities She was one of the Founders of the West Seattle Art Club and of the Seattle Milk Fund. The house was commissioned by Loveless in 1915 and the house was completed in 1917. The house is designed in combination of Colonial and Craftsman. It was positioned on the lot sideways where the living room and primary bedroom/sunroom are faced east towards the Seattle skyline. The front door is positioned on the side of the property and has classic stained glass windows. The proportions of the house are spacious with Craftsman detailing such as the Batchelder tiled fireplace surrounded by built-in bookcases with leaded paned glass doors. The staircase features a wide landing with Paladin windows and wood turned banister. The dining room is at the west side of the house with built-in cupboards with leaded paned glass doors. The kitchen was updated and a set of doors in the dining room leads out to the back yard where a pool and guest house have been added.

This West Seattle residence has an upper sunroom with view of the Seattle skyline.

Sunporch on upper level with views of the Seattle skyline.

Opposite: The Craftsman tile fireplace surrounded by built-in bookcases and French doors is the centerpiece of the living room.

Dining room with built-in hutch and original radiator boxes.

King / Wells Residence

1928

MAGNOLIA NEIGHBORHOOD

Mary Ann Wells was a well-known dance teacher at the Cornish School and later Director of the Mary Ann Wells School of the Dance. She was born in 1895 in Wisconsin. In 1916, she was invited by Nellie Cornish of the Cornish School to teach dance and founded the ballet department. In 1918, she married Albion Forest King who supported her career. In 1923, she opened her own dance school. Over the years, many of her students went on to fame, including Robert Joffrey who founded the Joffrey Ballet. She also taught ballroom dancing at the Women's University Club, Seattle Tennis Club and at the Church of the Epiphany.

Albion and Mary hired Loveless to design their Tudor revivalist home in 1927 and receipts show an estimated cost of $10,000. The property has a stucco exterior with a multi-pitched roof line, leaded pane glass windows and a sweeping view of Puget Sound and the Olympic Mountains. The witch character weathervane on the pitched roof was installed by Mary Wells and is still visible. Today, the lower level retains the dance studio designed by Mary Wells with mirrored walls and dance bars. Loveless himself painted a rooster mural in the studio that is still visible.

The "witch" weather vane was installed by Mary Wells, one of the original owners.

Entry front door is subtle which is a consistent Loveless architectural design detail used in many of his projects.

Arched hallway steps down to take in panoramic Sound views. This formal living room is located at the rear of the home to take advantage of the expansive views.

Magnolia Bungalow
1923

MAGNOLIA NEIGHBORHOOD

Little is known about the original resident of this Magnolia home that is located very near the entrance to Discovery Park. The home is located on a double lot with lush landscaping and charming garden spaces. The steep pitched roof lines and extensive dormer leaded glass windows are signature Loveless details. In subsequent years, a bump out turreted dining room and a bonus room were added as well as an enlarged and upgraded kitchen.

Built in 1923, this Loveless home sits on a double lot creating huge garden spaces and privacy. It has multiple leaded windows and cedar siding. Pitched roof lines and abundant windows are Loveless features.

The house features a radiator box bench, leaded pane glass windows and French doors leading out to brick patio, as well as a refined fireplace with Craftsman tiles, wood mantel and sconces.

Sparkman Residence

1909

QUEEN ANNE NEIGHBORHOOD

One of the early Seattle residents, James M. and Ida Sparkman came to Seattle in 1882. James was involved in the lumber business until 1890 at which time he partnered with Sutherland McLean to found one of the earliest real estate firms in Seattle. That same year he married Ida G. Ross, the daughter of John Ross, another prominent Seattle pioneer and farmer. In 1910, he and Ida moved into their Wilson/Loveless designed home. Subsequent owners have included influential fundraisers who hosted functions for presidential candidates at the home.

Grandly perched on its corner lot in Queen Anne, this house is almost completely hidden from the street by foliage creating a private enclave. A large formal entry with pocket doors leads to the living room and a sunporch that overlooks exterior pool. Balustrades and beamed ceilings are common design details for that time. Original windows feature oversized arched windows with leaded mullioned patterns.

The Sparkman Residence is located in the Queen Anne neighborhood and sits in seclusion and privacy. This house was a collaboration with Wilson.

The sunroom with curved windows overlooks the pool. The sunroom was originally open and was later enclosed with the deck added above.

A large entry with classic detailing of paneled walls, inlaid wood floor trim, pocket doors, and push-button light switches. The doors open up to formal living and sunrooms.

Boxed beam ceilings, inlaid hardwood floors and French doors create classic elements of the home.

The family room is flooded with daylight from the abundant classic windows.

The curved custom mullioned windows are an architectural detail of this large home.

Residential Designs

Broadmoor

Capitol Hill

Anderson Residence

1908

BROADMOOR NEIGHBORHOOD

This beautiful Spanish revival home is in the exclusive Broadmoor community and was designed for Dr. Roger and Susan Anderson. Roger Anderson was born in 1892 in St. Paul Minnesota. He was a private practice physician and resided here at least through 1942.

The home has detailed Spanish tile work, wood beams and smooth stucco interior walls throughout. The entry's arched double doors and a tiled staircase with curved wrought iron handrails are prominent features as you enter the home. Arched windows in the entry overlook the original Moroccan fountain courtyard. A step-down living room, atrium and updated outdoor fresco patio overlook the golf course. A covered portico leads past a second courtyard and connects to the detached garage with living quarters which were added later but were designed to blend effortlessly with the original design.

Entry foyer with arched wood double doors, tile floors, original wall sconces and wrought iron handrail.

The entry boasts double arched wood doors and large curved leaded glass window overlooking front courtyard with original Moroccan tile water fountain. Loveless travelled to Morocco and picked up the local influence. Step-down sunken living room from the tiled front entry hall. Original wood doors and trim. Walls are smooth stucco. The iron chandelier is original.

Arched entry window frames the original Moroccan tile fountain.

Lower level tiled staircase. Stucco walls and wrought iron handrails.

Atrium with beveled leaded glass windows

Bloch Residence
1908

CAPITOL HILL NEIGHBORHOOD

William Bloch immigrated to Seattle from Germany in 1889. In 1908, Wilson and Loveless designed their grand new home near Volunteer Park on Capitol Hill where William lived with his wife Minna and two sons. Bloch was a prosperous businessman and owner of the Germania Hall and Café. It was located downtown at Second and Seneca from 1905 to 1916. It was a common gathering place for local people of Germanic ancestry and featured a gymnasium, boxing ring, office space, and café that featured beer from the Seattle Brewing Company. It also held the Lois Theatre which was backed by Alexander Pantages. Until prohibition, the Café was a very popular watering hole. In February 1916, Seattle began to ban establishments such as the Germania from the sale of beer and wine and Bloch's business suffered due to prohibition and WWI. The family sold their house in 1918 and moved to Chicago. Bloch later returned to Seattle where he died in 1931.

The Bloch residence is an example of a Tudor Revivalist style with medieval influences. The 7520 sq.ft. home has 5 bedrooms and 4 baths. The exterior features a brick façade with half-timber/stucco detailing, heavy oak front doors and lead paned windows. Angled English chimney stacks are prevalent details. Many original features in the interior rooms remain including herringbone patterned oak floors, classic wood paneling, quarter sawn-oak pocket doors, and five fireplaces featuring varied patterned Craftsman tiles. Today, the original ballroom on the 3rd floor has been converted into a large library. It features original bench seating under roof eaves that were visiting areas during dances. The mural painted on the ceiling is a replica of ceiling in Grand Central Station in New York City.

The Bloch mansion was designed by Wilson and Loveless in 1909 in a Tudor Revivalist style. The original ballroom is located in the center room with the dormers.

Opposite: One of 5 fireplaces, with original copper-colored iridescent tiles with orignal Germanic mural above that was restored.

Built-in benches, boxed beam ceilings and pocket doors are original features of the home.

Commercial grade kitchen was originally used to serve large hosted events at the house. Today, commercial components still remain with William Morris Arts and Crafts wallpaper. Back stairwell leads to upper floors and ballroom/library

The hand painted mural is based on the mural painted at the New York Grand Central Station.

This reading room has pocket doors and is located off the main entry. The fireplace was constructed with Batchelder tiles and is surrounded by built-in bookcases. This room invites you to drop off your coat and stay awhile.

This sitting nook was designed for visitors to engage in small talk during dances which were held in the 3rd floor ballroom (which has been converted to a library). How many couples found true love off the ballroom floor in this alcove?

Residential Designs

Washington Park

Seward Park

Mt. Baker

Corbet Residence

1925

WASHINGTON PARK NEIGHBORHOOD

Loveless was commissioned by prominent Seattle businessman Darrah Corbet to design this AIA award-winning English Tudor style home in Washington Park. Darrah was President of Smith Canning Machines. Darrah and wife Katherine Corbet resided there until about 1969 when it was purchased by Fran Weisfield of Weisfield Jewelers.

The property sits at the end of a private dead-end lane with views of Lake Washington. Loveless was awarded the American Institute of Architects (AIA), Washington Chapter, Honor Award for "Dwellings of More than Ten Rooms" in 1928 and for the attractive use of brick and wood detailing with stone accents.

The entry is striking with a heavy wooden door with a Juliet balcony directly above the front entrance. Design motifs repeated throughout the house are bas relief grape motifs with leaves. Window features are leaded panes with a central stained window and intentional "cracks" in the corners of the window that Loveless designed with a level of whimsy. The tiled central hallway runs the length of the house and ties each room throughout. A small library with fireplace is a feature along with a grape motif tiled fireplace in the dining room. A series of arched hallways, arched doors and windows throughout the house is consistent. The rear exterior features a brick patio.

This AIA award-winning design is an outstanding example of romantic Tudor revival style that Loveless was well known for.

106

Above Left: Upstairs landing original wood handrail. Gothic arched doorways throughout with custom arched leaded glass doors.

Above Right: Dormer window features leaded glass window with stained glass insert of a sailing ship.

Opposite Top: Multiple dormered windows, and a pitched shake roof, leaded windows and a Juliet balcony are directly above the front entrance. A variety of brick pattern designs with a grape leaf motif adorn the entrance of the front door.

Opposite Bottom: Stained glass inserts depicts girl flying a kite next to front door. Door opening with iron detailing and original hardware.

Right: The same grape leaf motif seen at the front entry is also seen on the dining room fireplace.

Eckstrom/Canning Residence
1914

WASHINGTON PARK NEIGHBORHOOD

Lucille Eckstrom was born in Idaho in 1892 and came to Seattle where she attended the University of Washington (Class of 1915). She lived with an uncle and was on the staff of the UW Daily newspaper. She purchased the land in 1913 and the house was built in 1915. She married Achille B. Canning in 1917. From 1917-1921, the Cannings lived in Cleveland, Ohio. During that time, the house was occupied by John A. Porter who later had Arthur Loveless design his Mt Baker home. Achille Canning was a traveling salesman with the Scott E Bird Company and starting in 1922 they returned to the house on High Lane where they remained until 1926.

The House today still offers many original details in the entry, wood staircase, spacious living room with marble fireplace and dining room. The entry of the home has a private bricked courtyard behind a fence and the front door features an arched porch cover. The living room, dining room and terrace are positioned at the back of the property to take advantage of the views of Lake Washington. The kitchen has been updated and the master bedroom offers sweeping views. The primary bath has been renovated with a large walk-in closet.

Private bricked courtyard is the entry to this Washington Park property, with curved covered entryway and patterned cedar siding.

Entry way with views to front courtyard patio. The staircase is centrally located with views into the dining room and Lake Washington.

Although the bathroom has been updated, the classic elegant feel with ample light is consistent with Loveless' original intention

Opposite: The original fireplace with wood mantel has been updated with marble facing.

Brady Residence
1927

WASHINGTON PARK NEIGHBORHOOD

Hugh Brady was born in 1891 in Sitka, Alaska, the son of John Green and Lizzie Patton Brady. His father, John, was the 5th Governor of the District of Alaska (1896). Hugh was a graduate of Yale University. He married Mary Somerville Scheiffelin in March of 1931. Brady worked his way up in several lumber companies, eventually becoming President of several including the Colby Lumber Co. He was also Treasurer of the Brady & Ketcham Lumber Co and Kitsap Roofing. He founded Brady International Hardwood Company, Brady International Lumber, Inc and Brady Lumber Company. He organized the first Yale Enrollment and Scholarship Committee in Seattle in 1937. He was presented with the Yale Medal in 1952. Brady was a trustee of the Washington Forestry Conference, and a past president of the Washington Conservation Society.

He was a fellow of Davenport College at Yale University, a member of the Zeta Psi Fraternity, the University Club, Seattle Tennis Club, the Washington Athletic Club, and the Seattle Yacht Club. He was a founder and member of the Corinthian Yacht Club.

The architecture is traditional English cottage with arched shutters and mullioned windows that sits back on the lot creating a large front yard. The floorplan features an entry with staircase and a circular floorplan. The formal rooms offer spacious proportions with views of Lake Washington. The kitchen has been updated and extended. A lovely terrace and backyard offer sweeping views of Lake Washington and the Cascade Mountains.

This Washington Park classic carriage home was designed by Loveless to take advantage of the sweeping views.

Views of Lake Washington from the formal living room.

Formal spaces complement the traditional floorplan.

Yates Hickey Residence
1927

WASHINGTON PARK
NEIGHBORHOOD

Yates Hickey was born in 1886 in Pennsylvania. He was an agent for State Farm Insurance. His wife Margueretta was active in social circles. Built in 1927, the Hickeys were still there in 1951. He died in 1963 at the age of 77. He was a member of the Rainier Club and former member of the Union League Club.

The house is an English Cottage style with deep pitched roofline, dormer windows, shake roof and rose-tinted stucco exterior siding. Shutters and a river rock fireplace and an expansive terrace overlooked sweeping views of Lake Washington before the house was demolished in 2020.

Steps down into the large living room with views to the dining room. Wood paneling, built-in shelves, and French doors were key elements of the home.

Fireplace in living room had large custom wood paneling.

Fireplace in primary bedroom included classic Tudor revival detailing with stone and wood flanked by original brass wall sconces.

Palmer Residence

1927

SEWARD PARK NEIGHBORHOOD

This waterfront estate was originally owned by Dr. and Mrs. Don Palmer. Donald Palmer was born in Lincoln, Nebraska and came to Seattle when he was 4 years old. He graduated from the University of Washington in 1899 and received his medical degree in 1903 from Rush Medical College, Chicago. While at the University he competed in football, basketball and wrestling and was especially known in track. He held a record in the Pacific NW track scoring record having scored six 'firsts' in one meet. Dr. Palmer took the post of team doctor at UW in 1904 and resigned in 1947. He refused payment for his services at the university during all those years. He originated the Big W Club made up of students who win major athletic awards. He was a member of the King County Medical Society, the WA State Medical Association and the American College of Surgeons. He was a founder of the American Board of Plastic Surgery, a member of the Church of the Epiphany and chairman of the board of trustees of the Pioneer Association of the State of Washington. He was also a member of Phi Beta Kappa and Phi Rho Sigma honorary fraternities. He was a Mason, a member of the Nile Temple and a charter member of the Washington Athletic Club. Maude Palmer was a founding member of the Lake Washington Garden Club and the Arboretum Foundation. She was active in the Sunset Club, the Seattle Garden Club, the Church of the Epiphany, the Dr. Don Palmer Orthopedic Guild and a charter member of the Women's University Club.

Dubbed "WillowDon" by the Palmers, this Seward Park home has many of the classic Tudor Revivalist features of a Loveless home. Situated between the street and Lake Washington on a large tract of Lake Washington waterfront, it is oriented so the main living spaces have expansive views of the lake. The home boasts the stain glass ornaments embedded in the windows, arched doorways, crests, and multiple fireplaces. The gardens, originally designed by Olmsted Brothers, have been restored and expanded with above ground pools. A guest house with a 4 car garage was added to the property by a recent owner and stayed true to the design of the original house. The owners have a file of many of the original receipts for work done when the house was built.

Opposite: The compound sits on the shores of Lake Washington. Stucco exterior, slate roof tiles and Tudor stacked chimney.

One of several terraced lawns that lead to lakeside. This captures the two story bay window.

Above: The living room is accessed down steps. The room includes bookcase, central large ornate fireplace and leaded glass windows overlooking Lake Washington.

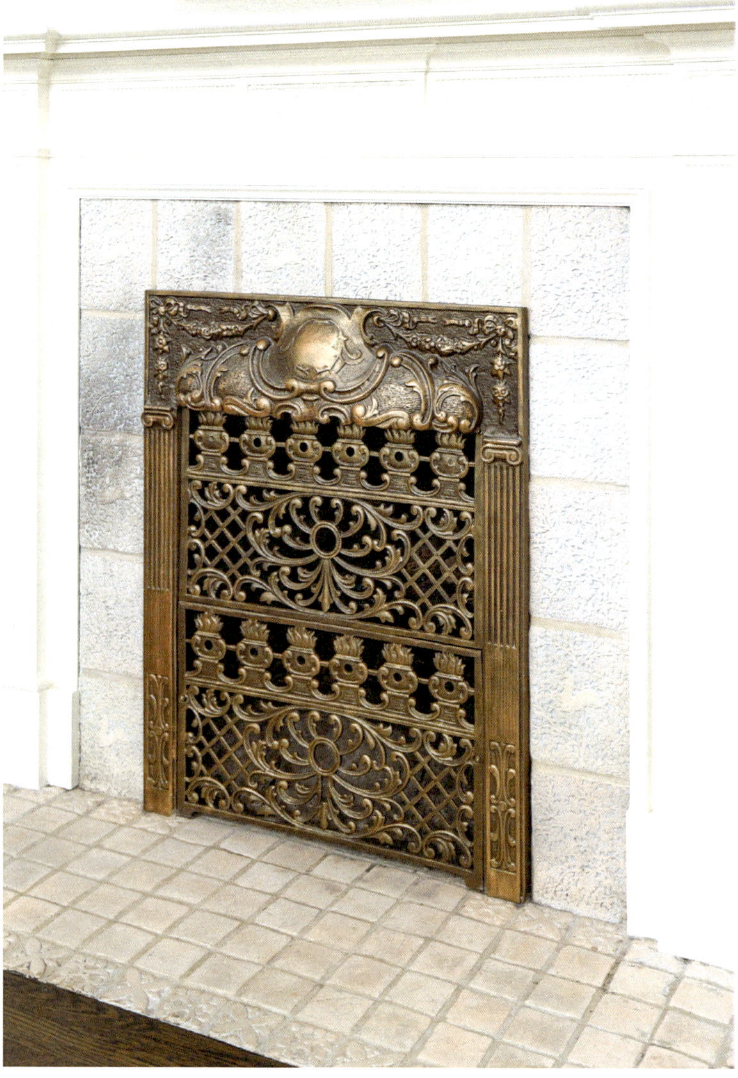

Left: The primary bedroom fireplace with original cast brass fireplace screen.

Above Top: Original Exterior Fish and Shell water fountain is built into the stucco siding. Located below the double height bay windows, it overlooks the large level grass area.

Above Bottom: A stained glass ship adorns a window.

A series of arches in upper hallway.

Pope Residence

1934

SEWARD PARK NEIGHBORHOOD

Designed for Edward and Katherine Pope, Edward was an Import Inspector and Secretary-Treasurer of Blake Moffitt Towne & Tombo. The home was subsequently sold to H.C. Converse, President of the Converse Company. This is one of the five two-acre tracts of land that Loveless and investors purchased on the shores of Lake Washington in Seward Park. Pope was one of the investors of the land development. It is known that Arthur Loveless was often on site to oversee the construction of this house. He personally selected many of the lumber pieces and other building materials that went into the finish work. The plumbing systems for its day were state-of-the-art and installed by Bowels Plumbing company (a Loveless client).

A 1934 Seattle Times article describes the home as "an English manor designed by Arthur Loveless. The English motif has been carried out with the utmost skill and care both inside and out. The house contains eleven rooms and three baths. A large basement recreation room opens onto the spacious lawn and garden." The house is a Tudor design with a stucco exterior, multi-pitched rooflines and dormer windows with leaded paned windows throughout. The lower level living room is spacious with views of the grounds leading to the waterfront.

Stucco exterior with multiple pitched roof-lines are classic Loveless designs.

The English cottage entry alcove with stained glass window and step down brick entry is a signature entry feature of Loveless.

Opposite: Beamed ceilings, built-in bookcases and wall sconces fill the room with charm.

Above: The wood paneling and fireplace are original.

Opposite: Dormer windows and step-up hallway levels create intimate spaces like this sitting area.

Arthur Loveless Residence

1925

SEWARD PARK NEIGHBORHOOD

Loveless spent $10,000 designing and building his personal residence on this 2 acre waterfront lot. He named it the "Hollyhock House" for the hollyhocks growing in the walled perennial garden near the front door. The house is a rambling English cottage style home with stucco exterior and interior walls, steep pitched roof lines and a shake roof. He installed grape leaf motif wallpaper in the dining room and the motif is in some of the stained-glass windows. Features of the house include ornate wood radiator boxes, French doors, and iron light fixtures. He designed the house with a main floor bedroom/bath suite for his parents who lived with him.

The Olmsted brothers designed the garden for Loveless as he was very involved in garden clubs and entertaining. In 1938, after the death of both of his parents and as he neared retirement, Loveless sold the home to William Hutchinson who founded the Fred Hutchinson Cancer Research Center.

Loveless was a fan of the grape leaf motif which he installed in the dining room of his personal home. The original embossed wallpaper has been painted over many times.

Opposite: Carved oak radiator boxes with leaded glass windows.

Stucco interior walls and original iron wall sconces.

Cozy nook with a bay window

Signature stained glass centerpiece with a small corner leaded glass "folly" to resemble a cracked window.

Opposite: Original curved French doors with leaded glass panes were removed from the main floor and placed in the entrance to the primary bath

John A. Porter Residence

1923

MOUNT BAKER NEIGHBORHOOD

John A. Porter worked his way up in the Frederick & Nelson Department stores, first as General Manager and finally as President. Between 1917-1922, the Porters rented the Loveless-designed Canning/ Eckstrom home until their home was completed at Mount Baker in 1923. It boasts wonderful views of Lake Washington. Subsequent owners hosted President Eisenhower during his 1956 campaign for his 2nd term where he was seen playing basketball with neighbor kids. When the current owners purchased the home, it had been remodeled in the 1950's fashion with picture windows and flat brick fireplace facades. The owners found the original Loveless blueprints and began to restore the house by changing windows back to leaded glass casement opening windows, window boxes, and Batcheleder Craftsman fireplace tiles and updated the kitchen and servants' quarters. The circular driveway and yellow front door are very inviting features of this home.

Classic proportions with a circular drive and a stucco exterior.

Opposite: Colorful entry door is a classic English Tudor entryway.

Major restoration based on original blueprints allowed owners to restore casement windows, doors and window boxes back to the house.

Kinzer Residence

1919

MOUNT BAKER NEIGHBORHOOD

Originally built for Phillip Kinzer who worked for the Carnation Milk Company, the home's more notorious owners were Roy and Elise Olmstead. During Seattle's prohibition years in the 1920s, Roy Olmstead became one of the largest and most successful bootleggers in King County. Learning how the trade operated from his experience in police raids and arrests while serving as a Seattle Police Lieutenant, Olmstead noted the lack of organization of many bootleggers and began his own operation. After an arrest and dismissal from the Seattle Police Force, he continued his operations which eventually grew to include many vessels, trucks, warehouses, and importing liquor from Canada. Along with his second wife, Elise, Olmstead established the American Radio Telephone Company which they operated from this home in Seattle's Mount Baker neighborhood from the second floor sunporch. It was suspected that the children's bedtime hour radio show was used to relay coded messages to the various rum-runners employed. Suspicious of the activities, federal agents employed illegal surveillance techniques and wiretapping to catch Olmstead. Olmstead found out about the wiretapping and would deliberately mislead FBI agents listening by sending them to false drop-off locations. Olmstead, his wife, and nine other men were arrested in 1924. After a Federal Grand Jury indictment in 1925, he appealed in a landmark case on the grounds that wiretapping was unconstitutional based on the 4th and 5th Amendments. After losing his appeal, Olmstead served four years' time at McNeil Island Penitentiary and was released in 1931. The wiretapping case law remains on the books today.

The interior of the house is much the same as it was when built with a split landing staircase with extensive windows. The lot is a level corner lot that has been upgraded with a sport court, and extended gardens. The enclosed sunporch where the radio show was hosted is still intact right off the primary bedroom.

From the backyard you can see the upper right sunporch where Elise Olmstead hosted her radio show.

Opposite: The staircase has curved oak banisters and a large landing.

The home has a large formal entry way with original wood trim.

The entry hall looks to the tiled sunporch overlooking the backyard.

Upper stair landing with custom built in bench.

Bowles Residence

1925

MOUNT BAKER NEIGHBORHOOD

Jesse Bowles graduated from Broadway High School in Seattle. He was President of his class at the University of Washington and graduated from Harvard University. He married Louise A. Collins in January 1917. Both Jesse and Louise were very active socially. Jesse worked in his father's wholesale plumbing company eventually becoming the president. He was also president of Northwest Envelope Manufacturing and secretary of Bowles & White Inc. He was active in the Seattle Yacht Club, holding a variety of officer positions. His wife, Louise, died in November 1940 from a back injury suffered 2 years prior when she fell through an open hatch on their yacht named Marilyn. Jesse then married Velda in October 1941.

The home is English Tudor style and is listed on the National Register of Historic Places based on its architectural design and construction. The Bowles property sits bluff side overlooking Lake Washington and is on a 32,000 square foot lot. The house itself is also large with over 8,930 square feet including separate servants' quarters.

The property is highlighted with multiple pitched shake roof lines, dormer windows and a central turret window overlooking the rear of the property. Brick, wood and half-timber materials are distinct details of the home. The large amethyst-colored stained-glass window panels in the staircase landing are a standout feature. The main entry hall is central to the grand staircase, views of the turret, and the large step-down living room.

The rear of the home features a three story turreted feature that captures views of Lake Washington.

Herringbone brickwork and grape bas relief detailing above the oak front entry door are a few of the classic detailing that Loveless was fond of implementing into his designs.

Colored stained glass windows are highlighted on the stair landing.

Loveless Gould Remodel

1914 / 1931

MOUNT BAKER NEIGHBORHOOD

Originally designed by Carl Gould in 1914, this Colonial design home was remodeled by Loveless in 1931. Multiple French doors are features on the ground floor with double crown molding, and circular floorplan. It has been updated throughout and still retains modern farmhouse finishes.

A series of French doors in the dining room and living room, pocket doors and crown moulding showcase classic detailing.

Craftsman tiled fireplace with detailed wood mantel.

Residential Designs

Windermere

Laurelhurst

Field Residence

1930

WINDERMERE NEIGHBORHOOD

Another of the 8 Colman/Loveless collaborations in Windermere, this home was designed for Henry Field, and wife, Marguerite.

Henry was born August 24, 1880 in Boston, Massachusetts and attended the Massachusetts Institute of Technology in 1903 before coming to Washington in 1904. In 1906 he was listed as President of North Coast Manufacturing, and by 1939 he was President of Pacific Lumber and Shingle Co. He married Marguerite White in 1912, described in the newspapers as a 'prominent social registrant and well-known welfare worker' who was involved in many charitable organizations.

One of the current owners is an interior designer who has created elegant living spaces while retaining many of the original details such as the knotty pine walls, windows, and fireplace. The proportions of the formal living spaces are spacious with views of Lake Washington as the focal feature of every room. The original Loveless blueprints highlight an ornate curved wrought iron staircase that was specified by Loveless, and it remains a design centerpiece of the entry today.

This Windermere home sits on a bluff overlooking Lake Washington.

Original pine-paneled den with Arts and Crafts tiled fireplace and built-in bar.

The wrought iron handrail was designed by Loveless and detailed in the original blueprints of the home.

Loveless designed the living room at the rear of the property to take advantage of the sweeping views. The room is adjacent to the library.

Bay widows with view of Lake Washington.

The views to the covered patio and Lake Washington are the focal point of this large entry hall (pictured opposite).

Although there is a huge entry hallway beyond, this arched doorway makes the space feel warm.

The entrance to the home is unassuming with an amazing view beyond.

Roebke Residence

1938

WINDERMERE NEIGHBORHOOD

This home was designed for Louis and Berenice Roebke. Born in 1891, he was a merchant at William Volker Co. in 1939 at the time the house was built, and still resided there in the 1950's while he worked at Martin Nelson & Co. The design is brick Georgain-esque, with black shutters and sweeping views of Lake Washington.

While the current owners have extensively renovated this home, the front of the house retains original features. Some Loveless design elements remain: the graceful balustrade, wood paneling, built-in bookcases, pink bath tiles, dining room layout with French doors leading to a large covered balcony. The kitchen and lower level have been extensively remodeled, and the backyard includes extensive updates with additions of a sport court, a covered balcony with exterior fireplace and an outdoor kitchen. The house overlooks Lake Washington.

The exterior of the home has undergone extensive remodeling to take advantage of the sweeping view of Lake Washington. A covered balcony with fireplace, and built-in outdoor kitchen overlook the level grass lawn and sport court.

The upstairs landing with curved banister and built-in storage.

Classic wood panel detailing, crown moulding and bookcases flank the marble clad fireplace.

Opposite: The pink tiles are original to the house.

Scripps Residence

1929

WINDERMERE NEIGHBORHOOD

James Scripps of the Scripps Publishing and newspapers fame was the first owner of the Norman revivalist architectural estate-like bluff home overlooking Lake Washington in the Windermere neighborhood. In 1941, ownership turned over to Lloyd Nordstrom of the Nordstrom store empire and remained a Nordstrom home until sold in 1969 to current owners.

In 1959 the house was included in the Seattle Art Museum's Ninth Annual Architectural Exhibit. The Times said "it carries out the theme 'Vintage Years' in celebration of the Art Museum's silver anniversary. The exhibit was a tour of ten Windermere homes.

The home features a large living room with beamed ceilings, a knotty pine-paneled library with a second staircase to upper-level bedrooms. The dining room ceiling has hand painted murals placed in between beams. The kitchen has been updated and has a large guest quarters located over the garages. The extensive property includes grounds with level patio and lawn with a tram leading to the lakefront beach.

This stucco and wood structure is located on 5 acres with a tram to the Lake Washington waterfront.

The library is tucked away at the back of the house which makes it feel like a private place. Note - original Eames chairs!

Large wood ceiling beams with hand painted designs in-between.

Step down into this intimate-feeling living room with beams

Pierce Residence

1928

WINDERMERE NEIGHBORHOOD

Designed for Frank Richardson Pierce and his wife, Vivian Grant Gill Pierce, this home was the first of 8 tracts built in Colman-Denny Windermere community with Lawrence Colman as developer and Loveless as designer. Pierce became one of America's more prolific writers, mainly Western stories. His career spanned nearly 50 years and produced over 1,500 short stories, 3 novels, and 4 feature films. He was owner of Forsberg Indian Company, Publishers.

Loveless designed the property with cross-gabled Tudor Revival styling, steeply pitched roofs and prominent projecting gables – two of which were half-timbered—on the front façade. The original cost of building the home was estimated to be $20,000.

After extensive deferred maintenance, the current owners hired restoration architects to update all systems, expand the front porch of the house, and add guest quarters over a rebuilt garage. A pool with paved patio offers sweeping bluff views of Lake Washington. An electric tram allows access to the lake front beach.

This Windermere home underwent extensive restoration to compliment Loveless design detailing. The front entry porch is an update to the original that had deteriorated over time.

Following pages: A pool with stone patio was added to create a seamless indoor-outdoor environment.

Windermere Tudor Revival

WINDERMERE NEIGHBORHOOD

While the original owner is unknown, this home was built on one of the eight lots that was developed by Colman and designed by Loveless. This property is a classic Tudor Revival design with a stucco exterior and multi-pitched rooflines and leaded pane bay windows and dormers.

Sprawling over 5 bluff view acres, the property is over 6000 sq ft with (originally) 7 bedrooms and 6 bathrooms. The room proportions are large and classical. The living room with fireplace, the dining room with French doors plus main floor family room off the kitchen area are all facing the view of Lake Washington.

Adjacent to the living room is a wood paneled study with an original fireplace. While this home has been modernized and updated, it retains the classic layout of a Loveless home. The grounds are extensive with access to a dock at lakeside.

The modern marble floors add a sense of modern glamour to the home. The latest extensive renovation in keeping with the times and the latest in materials without compromising character.

Entering the library provides a different feel. Notice the transition back to wood floors. This is a classically-proportioned room with a bank of windows on the right allowing in plenty of light. Even the radiator box gets a special treatment in this space.

Another signature Loveless design is making specific large rooms feel spacious and small rooms to feel cozy.

This arched bedroom entry is another great example of a Loveless transition. He wanted the bedrooms to feel cozy and intimate within the big house

Franklin Residence

1929

LAURELHURST NEIGHBORHOOD

George Franklin moved to Seattle from Texas where he had been the President of Tri-State Grocery Association. In 1929-1930 he attended the University of Washington at the same time as his son. He developed a chain of grocery stores in Tacoma and served as President of the Tacoma Philharmonic.

Loveless designed the house on the upper bank of Lake Washington in Laurelhurst. With a sloped yet sweeping lawn, a trail of switchbacks was created to get to the dock with enclosed swimming area and a boathouse. The interior of the home is distinctly French Norman revival with white-washed brick siding and French shutters. The entry has an ornate French door split entry, barrel vaulted ceiling in the kitchen eating nook with built-in cabinet. Wood trim, fireplaces and crystal door handles are other signature features in the home.

Split entry style with double doors and ornate leaded glass windows strategically-placed at andles allow the resident or guest to take a moment before entering.

This home was built into the side of the hill.

These are two examples of Loveless signature transitions. Intimate doorways, steps up and down in and out of rooms allow for the owner or visitor to transition from space to space.

The kitchen eating area has a barrel vaulted ceiling and built-in bookcase.

Opposite: French Normal revival details include whitewashed brick, French shutters and a copper clad bay window and door.

Residential Designs

View Ridge

Sheridan Heights

Shelton Residence
1939

VIEW RIDGE NEIGHBORHOOD

The original owners were Mary and Celia Shelton. They were both listed as members of The Mountaineers, a local outdoor recreational club. Their home was one of the last Loveless designed before retirement and reflects a newer Northwest style of colonial home.

Typical of many Loveless homes, the entry is understated with the back side of the house designed to take full advantage of the view. It has been thoroughly updated and remodeled inside.

Although some alterations were made to this property, the original cedar siding and rooflines remain.

Additions to the house were made with maximizing views

The brick fireplace and mantel is original to the house built in 1938.

Lush greenery and sweeping views of Lake Washington.

Street of Dreams

1938

SHERIDAN BEACH NEIGHBORHOOD

The architectural project in Sheridan Heights was a five-home project, undertaken with joint sponsorship of the Bon Marche, Puget Mill Company and the Seattle Trust & Savings Bank. The project, with designs by 5 different architects, would attempt to make full use of the Puget Sound area's climate, scenic and environmental advantages and feature new building methods. The main architectural elements of the home were distinctly art deco with streamlined detailing in handrails and window trim. Today, updated kitchen and bonus area have views of the north end of Lake Washington. Loveless' model was sent to the Golden Gate International Exposition for display in the Homes and Garden section.

Besides Loveless, the other participating architects were all well known in Seattle: William J. Bain, George Wellington Stoddard, Edwin J. Ivey (whose home featured the new 'dry wall') and J. Lister Holmes.

Thousands of people turned out to view the 1940 Street of Dreams open houses. All the homes were billed as a Northwest take on the colonial style home.

The varied building materials and different style are on display as soon as one enters the courtyard Wood above, stucco below, and unique front door detailing all give this home a very unique feel.

Garden windows even with new materials and a new style, are signature Loveless elements

The fireplace pictured far right is also a departure in terms of materials (although the immediate right is what we might expect), but coupled with a room transition with step down into the living room is Loveless through-and-through

Residential Designs

Woodway Park/Edmonds

Bainbridge Island

Bloxon Residence
1928

WOODWAY PARK
NEIGHBORHOOD

Built for Merritt Bloxon, this residence boasts many architectural details equated with Loveless' work. It is designed as an English Tudor country estate sitting on several acres. With a sweeping driveway, the home was constructed with a turret, Juliet balcony, wood paneling, arched doorways and situated so that the main living spaces are situated at the rear of the property. A large patio and lawn at the rear of the home lead to a bluff with views of Puget Sound, Whidbey Island and the Olympic Mountains. Restoration and updates have been extensive including restored ceiling panel details, wood paneling, restored dining room details and an updated chef's kitchen.

202

This home has amazing ceiling panels throughout - in the public spaces as well as the private. Dark wood accent paneling makes it feel very homey and intimate despite it being a sprawling estate.

On these pages we also see a number of transitions from space to space, each one with a focal point inside to draw you in further.

Frederick & Lucille Fischer Residence

1916

BAINBRIDGE ISLAND

In 1917, Fischer Brothers incorporated as a wholesale grocery located on Western Ave in Seattle. Frederick and his brother George ran the business. Frederick was Vice President and after George passed away in 1924, Frederick took over as President. In 1920 Fred was an Executive Committee member of the Alaska Bureau of the Seattle Chamber of Commerce along with James Haight (another Loveless home-owner). Frederick married Lucille Chapin in 1918 who was a prominent social and charitable leader. He and Lucille were avid travelers. In 1938 while visiting Auckland New Zealand, Frederick passed away and Lucile sold the house shortly thereafter.

The residence sits on one of the most recognizable locations on Wing Point on Bainbridge Island. This home and waterfront property is visible from the ferry as you enter Eagle Harbor ferry dock. The house was originally clad in cedar shingles in a neoclassic design. Original quarter sawn-oak paneling and detailing remain throughout today. Built-in benches and paneled walls are also present. The Arts and Crafts fireplace has original tiles. A sunporch that was originally open was enclosed at some point. The exterior has multiple pitched rooflines, dormers and a dormered eating area off the kitchen. The original staircase handrails and built-in bookcases are still intact. A porch overlooking the harbor allows close up views of ferries as they enter and leave the harbor.

Wing Point is an iconic location on Bainbridge Island.

The second set of steps with glass door is to a once-open sunroom that is now enclosed.

The home features close up views of ferry arrivals and departures.

Ceiling beams, built-in book cases, and quarter sawn-oak paneling are all original.

Original 1916 Craftsman-tiled fireplace.

Susan Shorett
Author

Susan's passion for architecture and history is the driving force behind this collection. Since the late 1890s, five generations of Susan's family have called Seattle home. Her great-great-grandparents moved to Alki beach as settlers and her family still lives on Alki Beach today. Her family also has long time ties to Edmonds and Kingston. And, of course, her great-great-uncle was the well-known Arthur Loveless, builder of notable homes in some of Seattle's earliest neighborhoods.

It was through her family that her passion for history and vintage homes flourished. In 2005, she undertook a "Rehab Addict" renovation of a 1901 log home (pictured in the postcard on the following page). She has also renovated a 1906 Craftsman, a 1918 Bungalow, and a 1960 mid-century ranch home. She is connected to the community and historic societies helping people purchase specific period homes, and is familiar with local artisan tradespeople who specialize in different period renovations.

Creating a documented collection of her ancestor's great contributions to Puget Sound architecture turned from idea to completed work in a few short years under Susan's guidance. Her vision, excitement, and project-management skills were critical tools in bringing this book to fruition.

Real estate is where tradition meets change. There is no secret to why Susan selected real estate as her choice in career. Houses are always exciting and fun to explore! Each holds a history behind the walls and she finds it a challenge to match the home with its next steward.

Susan IS the Puget Sound's Vintage Home Expert!

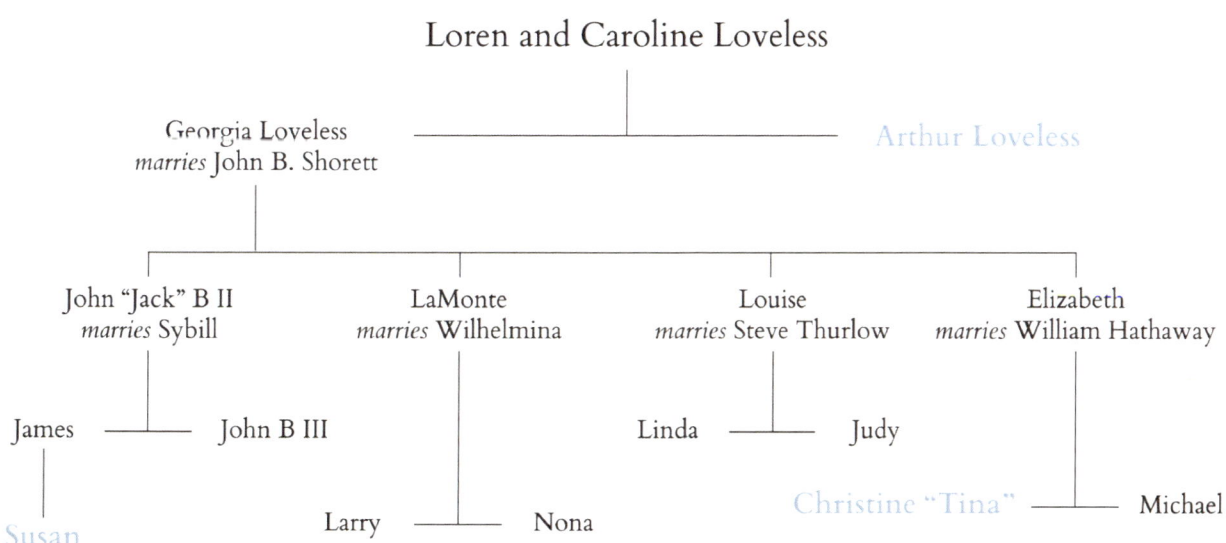

As you may have surmised, creating this book and documenting the works of such a master architect has been a passion project of the authors. Below is a family tree that links authors Susan Shorett and Tina Tyler to Arthur Loveless.

Loren and Caroline Loveless

- Georgia Loveless *marries* John B. Shorett
- Arthur Loveless

Children of Georgia and John B. Shorett:

- John "Jack" B II *marries* Sybill
  - James — Susan
  - John B III
- LaMonte *marries* Wilhelmina
  - Larry — Nona
- Louise *marries* Steve Thurlow
  - Linda — Judy
- Elizabeth *marries* William Hathaway
  - Christine "Tina" — Michael

Tina Tyler (Christine)
Researcher

According to Tina, her life has been one of shallow roots but stout branches. She was the only child in the Hathaway-Shorett family born outside of Seattle. Her paternal grandfather was a draftsman and maternal grandfather was a well-known Seattle attorney, John B. Shorett, known as 'the Father of the Duwamish.' Tina remembers most holidays spent with some of the family. As her parents drove into Seattle, her mother would point out various homes and buildings that had some family history attached to it. Her 'home' felt larger than just her house as Seattle was part of their family's history.

Over the years Tina had collected pictures, stories, and memorabilia which were stored in her father's military footlocker. Sorting through the history of her ancestors, expanding the family tree in Ancestry.com, and chasing down the links to find more information became a passion project of Tina's. She had just about finished when, at a family gathering, she reconnected with Susan Shorett, the daughter of her cousin, Jimmy. Susan shared Tina's interest in family history and shared with Tina the interest of wanting to create a collection of their shared relative's works. She enjoyed getting back into research mode in support of the project.

Tina made one last move (with the help of her real estate cousin Susan Shorett)! They now live in Port Angeles which embodies so many of the things Tina loves in the northwest – mountains, water, boats, mild weather, and family.

@tina.tyler2

Eric Dennon
Photographer

Eric is celebrating over 20 years in the photography industry specializing in photographing products, people, and architecture. Every project's uniqueness provides him the opportunity to find that great shot, angle, or develop a professional relationship. Crafting compelling images that capture a property's unique essence is what has kept Eric top of mind in the industry.

Susan met Eric through his real estate photography work and knew he had the perfect eye for this book project. Once they began to discuss the scope of the project, they realized they had their work cut out for them with 75 unique homes and structures identifed. Through coordination and the openness of many Loveless homeowners they were able to photograph 37 of these homes and captured the unique characteristics Arthur brought to each home design.

With many of the homeowners being great stewards of their homes, maintaining much of the original home style, this gave Eric an opportunity to showcase the Tudor Revivalist and Spanish Colonial Revivalist styles. He found it very exciting to spend time in these special homes and really absorb the intention of Arthur's design. Once all the homes had been documented, it was then time to dive into the final process of refining the collection of images. This was a special joy and honor for Eric as he became the photographic steward of these very special historic homes.

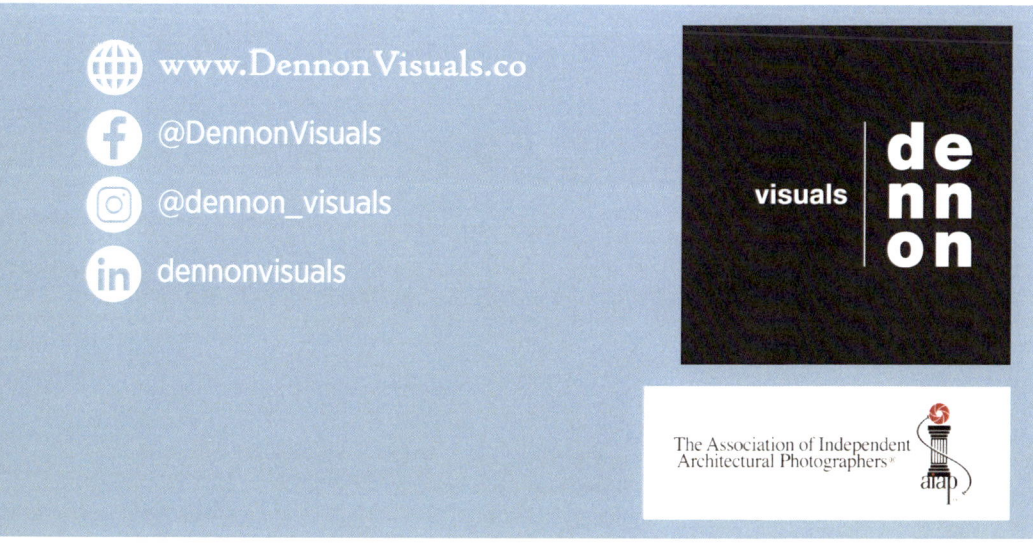

The authors, contributors, and sponsors are grateful for the Loveless homeowners who lovingly opened their homes for us to photograph. Without them, this book would not have been possible.

John and Sallie Chaney

Jessica and Tom Hughes

Dan and Theresa Evans

Brad and Corey Lovering

Maryanne Tagney and David Jones

Carolyn and Lindsey Echelbarger

Curt and Paula Green

Mary-Alice Pomputius and Walter R. Smith

Bob and Lisa Ratliffe

Peter & Sharlee Eising

Zig and Stephanie Burzycki

www.ingramcontent.com/pod-product-compliance
Lightning Source LLC
Chambersburg PA
CBRC091209010526
44107CB00022B/1268